Dario Asplanato

PHANTOM CONSCIENCE

2018

Global Vision Project

Preface

This book is dedicated to young and very young people, it is written in simple words and talks about humanistic and scientific themes.

It is not a philosophical treatise but rather tries to give points for reflection on very practical issues that every boy or girl, growing up, must face.

Do not take things for granted, it is a first step for inner growth and allows the development of high awareness and balanced personality.

This book was created with the intention of offering a different approach and a new perspective to the meaning that each of us gives to words as Life, Religion, Love, Sex, Politics.

It is not divided into chapters but only for arguments, continuing the scan play for, all the others will follow a common logical thread.

The whole book is built on the assertion that the phrase "I have conscience, therefore I exist " is false.

By contrast the phrase "I think, therefore I am", is true.

The meaning of the first argument is fundamental to continue reading.

Thought and Conscience

The first thing to understand about ourselves is who or what we are.

The body that houses it is the species homo sapiens, and is in effect, an animal, we tend to forget it because our conscience feels different.

It is a common mistake, really is our conscience not to be present in other animals.

The body has its specificities but remains an animal.

The body inherit that is not ours, this is another common mistake when we refer to the "our body", in reality the body is our father and our mother own.

If you look in the mirror, you should recognize the physical evidence of what i say.

You should easily recognize the characters of your mother and/or father's face.

Not inherit only the external features but also the flaws and benefits of the bodies of our parents.

Without haste or anxiety, you learn how to better manage what until now you thought were your body and write down your "instruction manual".

If your parents you will stare with wide eyes not let scruples and seek advice from their treating physicians.

Joke. now you are young and you think not, but the advice that my conscience obliges me to give you is that you discover if you suffer from possible hereditary diseases, allergies or other but also positive things as immunity and specific antibodies.

You may have inherited a body that has the anxiety of your mother or your father's teeth, which is never a decayed tooth in his life.

If you can become aware that the body is not yours, you may pick you want to find out when you will have it.

The answer seems simple, when you have a child .

The problem is that you can not live there because it is already occupied by another consciousness . that your child .

The consciousness and the body that houses it, are different in nature.

4

A body is any animal or vegetable or mineral as a stone, in order to exist needs a mass, to have a weight.

To have a space to occupy and time to acclimate.

The famous scientist Albert Einstein has put together these conditions with the formula $E = m c^2$ that one day you will study and understand.

For the moment, suffice it to say that consciousness, that each of us, is pursuing a body that can't reach.

Consciousness has no body, so it has no weight and can't exist nor be alive.

Not yet.

But every one of us think! is not possible that we do not exist!

I think therefore I am!

True, if you think, is there, in fact there is also an animal, manages to think, to move, to stop, to play, to hunt.

Conscience is to know of thinking.

If a sloth could say "I think therefore I am" manifest a consciousness and homo sapiens could become a big problem.

In the wild, animals can think exactly like us.

I can define "chemical thinking" dictated by the brain matter that manages it.

That handles so each animal also each of us.

Recapitulate:

We think we are alive but it is not true.

We think we have a body but it is not our.

Or when we will have one, it will be occupied by another consciousness.

Consciousness does not exist, but each of us is identified with it.

So, we do not exist.

The thought does not identify ourselves because even the rabbits think.

Homo sapiens that hosts us could live without us "conscious thought"?

The answer is yes, we are not required to homo sapiens, we have taken possession of an animal species with the evolutionary step by step.

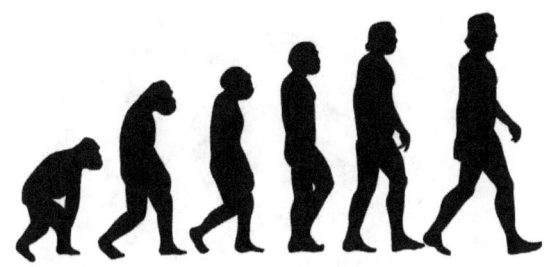

Now I will try to make you see the difference between animal thought and human consciousness with the image that is closest to the shape and substance of which we are made.

Of the phantom exists only the form.

The shape is the boundary of chemical thought, its frontier.

The chemical thought has deep roots in the mass/bed sheet and not on the form of the phantom.

An animal can be recognized in the bed sheet.

A consciousness recognizes itself in the phantom.

The phantom does not exist. manifests itself.

We are only protesters.

For me it is hard to explain it better than that.

Know that this book is centered on this issue and the next topics will try to confirm this thesis.

Some scientists have searched through experiments, to test the degree of consciousness in different animal species.

It might be useful to search the internet results of this research and compare them with my thesis.

In any case, learn to know you and to recognize where and how you are feeling more real.

Conscience is to know to think, recognize regardless of what is thought.

Thought exists in every animal, and is therefore alive.

If the thought is alive, it shall have a mass.

The smallest chemical thought, that you know, is the cell that generates another cell, so this small chemical thought is written in the DNA namely in the genetic code of the cell. It is an evolutionary capacity.

The complex chemical thought is, as I wrote, the frontier of the mass.

In any animal, the border of the mass is explored in the brain, composed of billions of cells.

Most likely, it is in the brain that are compiled changes to the genetic code to be transferred to the offspring.

The victory of a virus that could kill the parent, the renunciation of one of the five senses in favor of the greater sensitivity of another, the ability to jump higher or farther away, transforming the composition of muscles.

Are genetic information to be transferred to the offspring and the brain writes the results in the chemistry memory of the cells.

Evolution is the term that identifies the changes achievable by chemical thought.

Progress is the term that identifies the changes achievable by conscience in the social, political, scientific, economic and other ambits, not only in the human species but in the whole ecosystem.

So the thinking is still tied to matter and we can define it alive.

But if consciousness does not exist, then how manifests itself in the human species?

So how nature evolves creating questions and answers, action and reaction, cause and effect at the same time, part of the answer is in the question.

There is only the human brain, there are thousands of different species brains that have physical and chemical characteristics comparable to ours, and like ours, they use the chemical thought.

But they do not manifest consciousness.

To do this, a brain of a different species from ours should not only be made of the same substance, it should also recreate the same hierarchical structure of cells.

Structure is the term that identifies consciousness in the human brain.

A different hierarchical arrangement of cells, whose probability of combination, is equivalent to winning the lottery.

The human race only has to hope that no other living species on the planet will simmer such a combination.

If you have not seen the movie "Planet of the Apes" you can't understand what I'm talking about, so watch it.

The next topic is not lighter .

The Computer and the Animal

In this topic I look for all the analogies between our animal body and perhaps the most important invention of the human species.

Like a computer, an animal is born or turned on by withdrawing chemical energy from the mother and builds its body hardware.

DNA is the programming language used to hold BOOT information.

From a few initial cells the procedure written in DNA uses the combinatorial calculation to produce other cells that will build the entire fetus.

I explain as simply as I can.

In a cell that doubles or "gives birth" to a new cell, it remains a trace of being a mother.

The second cell registers that it is "daughter".

Between the two cells there is an electrochemical mutual recognition connection.

Not only does the "mother" cell communicate to the "daughter", but through the connections it succeeds in presenting the "grandmother" and so on.

As the cells split, the connections between them increase exponentially, but every cell can recognize its own condition and hierarchical position. therefore groups of cells will form a hand, others a foot etc. etc.

It seems incredible but all the communications and the connections between all the "relatives" cells follow a rigorous start-up program (BOOT) that is unchangeable, if it were you could be born with one foot instead of the hand..

So nature, cell after cell adds information and connections to transport them.

Nature adds (adds up) or takes away (subtracts), does not divide or multiply. This is another fundamental subject on mathematics that I will discuss later.

The brain is the most complex organ that in homo sapiens houses the consciousness, but in an animal it also hosts thought with a capital P allowed by chemical thought.

Billions of cells connected to each other by the chemical thought that can produce "free thought" that is not strictly bound to matter but dependent on it.

The frontier of thought, which records an infinite amount of information on the hard disc.

Some of them will become ROM (resident memory) and others will be deleted in RAM (rewritable memory).

The brain is the Processor.

Life.exe is the operating system.

Programs written in the DNA language are managed by chemical thought and are of the type heart.exe or lungs.exe.

Life.exe is the evolutionary system, it can make changes in cell programming by adding or removing information that will be transmitted to the offspring.

From the males, through the cells that make up the spermatozoa.

In females, through the cells that make up the oocytes.

Another topic.

Suffice it to say that free thinking is, in essence, how chemical thought and data acquisition peripherals work together.

Devices on a computer are like: the printer, the microphone or the webcam..

Our peripherals are heard, sight, touch, taste and smell.

As any hardware needs its drivers, so our peripherals are activated thanks to the system boot information.

Don't worry. If you fail, the system reboots and cuore.exe and polmoni.exe do not stop. The conscience vanishes but then reappears precisely because it is not alive and does not exist.

However think about it. If we do not exist, there are advantages. We can't die.

Another topic on theology and religions.

Let's continue.. with an affirmation on the conscience: the conscience is unique. . simply because it is a structure.

Each of us is distinguished from others only by the differences in the acquisition of data from the five senses, by the interpretations that free thought processes and makes writing chemical thought in memory.

Imagine that we are born without peripherals, free thought is empty, consciousness has no body .

Without sight . no light

Without smell . no perfumes

Without hearing . nothing sounds.

Without taste . no flavors.

But above all without tact . no space, or lack of mass perception . this sense is underestimated but it is what makes us individuals with a space / time . the touch is not only in the fingers but each of us also blindfolded, if he uses any part of the body, can recognize the objects "on the skin" only with the contact .

In these unfortunate conditions every human being has the same conscience.

Not just any but The Conscience . what scientists would define as an entity, that is something from which we derive. we comes.

Consciousness can't manifest itself. As soon as the drivers start working and the peripherals send data to be processed to the brain, the diversification begins between human beings and the appearance of Individual Consciousness.

Individual Consciousness begins to manifest itself and is what each of us perceives as "myself".

The computer and the animal have many other basic things in common and I will recall them in other topics.

Social Unconsciousness
and
Individual Conscience

The term Social Unconsciousness defines the state of evolution achieved by nature on the planet.

Social. because even if unconscious combines in a single evolutionary project all the matter of the universe and everything is interconnected by time and space.

Social Unconsciousness is the highest form of the evolution of life on planet Earth and naturally continues to evolve.

Animals belong to the world of Social Unconsciousness.

For convenience from now on I will use I.c. to define a human being and S.u. to define everything that has no conscience.

Someone might be tempted to define the S.u. world, like everything that was before the manifestation of the I.c. world, or the appearance of man.

Actually as the I.c. it does not exist, the world S.u. it is not influenced and continues its path.

Still using the analogy with the computer.

The Life.exe program is the only App that expands in memory and uses data from devices to power free thinking.

With the passage of time more and more data will be stored and made available at your request.

Life.exe acquires what the I.c. defines intelligence, or the union between memory, free thought, chemical thought and consciousness.

Life.exe in an animal does not develop intelligence.

Intelligence is a definition I.c. and is used improperly to define an animal.

Life.exe in an animal acquires faculty. These may or may not be used depending on whether the motivation coming from the outside world, elaborated by free thought, will be judged useful or not for the evolutionary process and therefore written by chemical thought.

The difference between animal faculty and intelligence I.c. it is the same between thinking and knowing to think.

The Life.exe program is as if it were written in binary language, that is, made of numbers 0 and 1 that turn on or off a memory value like a light switch.

Billions of cells in the brain send or hold information.

As in a computer the system can be defined as 8-bit or 64-bit (indicatively) depends on whether it is an insect or an elephant.

This is S.u. world.

Although the thought inherent in the logic of the Life.exe program can become complex and reach 128 bits or 32768 bits, it will never exceed the limits of the concept of True and False, of 0 and 1, of on and off, of living cell or dead.

Exactly like a computer.

Do you know why a robot will never reach self-consciousness?

Because it is built like an animal.

Dead or alive. True and False. 0 or 1.

Only if one day the I.c. it began to exist and implemented in a machine, for example, the value Doubt, in addition to True and False, could be defined as Conscious Creativity and robots could become the new bodies of I.c.

Immortal until the battery runs out.

You young I.c. maybe you do not remember the Star Trek series and their teleportation.

I always thought and now it seems safe that the teleportation of living matter is impossible.

But we are not "alive".

You will see that we will also fit well in a can.

So we are already used to virtual sex.

Joking aside, scientific research in a more precise and pompous way, is examining all the possibilities to define what conscience is and why it manifests itself.

Returning to Life.exe, it is a good idea to give some examples of how the animal computer works.

Life.exe manages, among other things, to move our body, to make us grasp the objects or allow us to tie our shoes.

This last action in a monkey, as in a man, requires that Life.exe develops in many bits.

That is, that the fundamental information, consisting of simple 0 and 1, are in large numbers and arranged in the right sequence to obtain the complex number of movements that the animal fingers must perform to fasten the laces.

Pay close attention to the next step that shows the difference between an I.c. and a S.u.

In nature, no animal is interested in lacing its shoes.

This sentence reads: nature addresses Life.exe on the purposes, in a logical and linear way. If the environment changes, the animal changes place or adapts itself through solutions generated by Life.exe and these solutions are very often just tentative measures.

Sometimes it seems that the solutions applied by an animal or even a plant are really ingenious.

In reality, the cause and effect have the same degree of difficulty or simplicity.

Now I want to make an extreme statement: if it is true that the I.c. it does not exist, then even everything that derives from it does not exist.

Look around and choose any object built by man.

Anyone.

In the world of S.u. nature would never have done it. But not only.

In the world of S.u. that object is not even recognized because it is realized with a non-linear logic made possible only thanks to the I.c.

Do you know the rhinoceros that is about to set up an off-road vehicle in Africa?

He sees him move, he hears him grumbling but he does not recognize him, it would be more consistent for him to be approached by a mass composed of iron oxide, silica, oil, etc. that is, from all the raw materials that compose it and which it could recognize as natural. Instead there is an object in front of it that not even nature knows what it is, the rhino starts charging and hits her, without anger, nor excessive violence, with curiosity, almost to want to test the nature, understand a cause and effect reaction.

Do you know the fly that wants to get out of the glass door of your building and is stubborn to give headboards or to scamper on that vertical transparency?

Do you think the fly is stupid?

I saw humans who, to get her out, they blew at him, they moved air with their hands, to help it they crushed her in a corner and it seemed almost like that, but then she would raise her head down against the glass.

I've seen humans take down the door or break the glass, and in the meantime talk to the fly "and go out, come on, you want to go".

Cause and effect same degree of complexity or simplicity.

Cause: fly against glass.

Effect: human who wants to help the fly out.

The more man struggles to get her out, the more the cause that blocks the fly is complex.

The solution appears simple, the fly flies to the light that draws the contours of what he knows, he knows that flying reaches his goal was also a dog shit.

If he runs into a spider web, he realizes he is trapped and struggles to death even if the spider does not show up.

Linear logical thinking generates action and reaction in events and situations that seem unrelated.

In nature, an old cobweb abandoned by the spider, favors the escape of the trapped insect, with the simple fact that if the cobweb is old, it has lost viscosity and toughness.

The fly agitates, breaks it, and flies away.

In the world of S.u. nothing is wasted, and everything is connected by linear thought, even if it seems more complicated when it takes on multi-directionality.

Returning to the glass, the fly does not even recognize it as an object, not only does not see it, but not being trapped "goes out" of its logical thinking, walks on it then seeks a passage, then flies, and fights against, the external landscape knows him, he would also know the threat of a spider's web, nature until the end, but what he has in front of him does not exist, it is not natural because he is a product of I.c. not of the S.u.

Only an external intervention unlocks the paranoia of the fly, only by opening the door, the fly no longer sees the external landscape and looks for it in another direction, or crosses the gap between the door and the wall, or by flying outwards, naturally the same situation would be repeated even with a little bird and the usual human would be able to say "but you do not see the glass, stupid!"

Fly and rhinoceros are examples of a single social unconsciousness.

Many books are now available, to deepen the subject on animal conscience in the world of S.u.

The research would seem to lead to clamorous conclusions, and it is useful for each of you, young I.c., to deepen these topics, know your animal body that hosts us, is essential for psychological balance, to decide what we will do as adults, and with what probability of success.

For the moment leave the house, if you are reading this book outdoors, look around.

The I.c. change the matter giving it unnatural forms, keep this in mind: the more the technology is advanced, the less the modification lasts over time.

One of the most enduring human works, which the I.c. he made our bodies realize, they are the pyramids.

Low technology, granite blocks laid one on top of another, good, thousands of years.

Almost all the less lasting works that the I.c. he did realize our bodies are contemporary, and the trend is accelerating.

We are making less and less things for our bodies and more and more things for our I.c.

To our body it is enough to eat healthy, to drink clean, to sleep well, to have a roof on the head, and to reproduce.

To us I.c., it is no longer enough, our body. Not being able to evolve, because we are not alive, we want to progress.

Because we can not exist, we take refuge in the virtual:
virtual reality, virtual friends, virtual trips, virtual currency, virtual sex, etc.etc.
Perhaps the movie Avatar is a rehearsal of exodus.
However we must always be present to ourselves and seek the truth: an incontrovertible truth is that nature, for example, does not multiply and does not divide, at least until the I.c. appeared, it added and subtracted, then, some animal became of affection, others have fastened their shoes, okay.

I.c. and Mathematics

Example: 10 rabbits.

In nature 10 rabbits can become 9 if one dies, so if 1 is subtracted.

Same thing if one is born, will be added, and become 11.

Human math says that if we take 5 rabbits and multiply them for 5 other rabbits, we get 25 rabbits.

In nature, there are always 10 rabbits.

Human math says that if we take 10 rabbits and divide them by 2, we get 5 rabbits.

In nature we get 10 dead rabbits.

Or at most 5 pairs of rabbits that hug tightly.

The numbers that humans define as natural, like 1, 2, 3, 4 etc. etc. by nature, they are up to the number 9, the number 10 is no longer recognized because defined with unity and zero. Put together by nature is absurd. unity can be a rabbit, a cell, or anyway an infinitesimal mass present in the universe, but zero is nothingness and nothingness does not exist, not in nature. Think of the border of the existing that should be the boundary of the universe. Imagine a grain of sand that goes beyond the existing one. Impossible, simply because with its presence, nothingness, it has moved away, nothingness is all that is not yet.

A mass, a hair, a rabbit that moves towards nothingness never reaches it, because it simply becomes.

Nothingness does not exist in nature and 1 rabbit divided 0 rabbits makes 1 rabbit, which is happy.

For humans and their mathematics makes endless rabbits, impossible, but there is a reason.

Simplification. Nature follows strict rules, no leaf moves that nature does not want.

Of God I will write later.

The I.c. have assumed the worldwide numerical decimal system.

The decimal system with the use of zero is a strong simplification.

With only nine numbers and zero you can write and calculate infinite numbers.

There is only one problem. In nature all numbers are prime numbers, there is no identical cell to another, simply because they occupy, for example, different space and time.

In nature there are no divisions but the I.c. have defined that prime numbers are those numbers that are divisible only for themselves or unity.

The prime numbers are all odd, except the number 2 and all seem to come out of the random decimal system, but the latest research seems to confirm that they are related to the presence of the number zero.

If you become a mathematician or a scientific researcher, you will have to study even the most unusual aspects like this: simplification, in the adopted mathematical language, makes it possible to find solutions to complicated problems, but at the same time generates problems without solutions, because a simplified language of reality is not the reality.

Example of paradox: in this book there is at least one error, this statement can only be true because if there are no errors the phrase "in this book there is at least one error" is an error.

All the mathematical paradoxes of the decimal system originate with the choice to use the number zero, and with it the simplification 1 divided by 0 equal to infinity.

In pure mathematical research, simplification generates distorting effects such that the corrections to be made are increasingly complex, and this is also a paradox.

However, simplified mathematics remains the material that we will use most in our life and, if we do not need to calculate a space / time gap, it is sufficiently precise.

I am aware of looking for a fixed point in this topic.

For Einstein's relativity a fixed point is a paradox.

You know the sentence: stop the world I want to get off.

Imagine running in the opposite direction to the rotation of the earth, imagine you are going so fast that you seem to stand still from the planet, then look up and see the sun and you realize that you are turning it around anyway. At this point it is necessary to change direction and speed, also to be stopped in relation to the sun. Continue to change direction and speed for each moving object in the universe until you reach a fixed point in relation to existence. At this point, stop existing and become a singularity. The black hole is one of the most famous singularities and if this my paradox was confirmed, the "fixed point" would be added to the singularities.

What I want to tell you is that the I.c. has enormous potential and at the same time disarming limits.

The I.c. does not exist, it can not intervene on evolution, but it can, thanks to progress, modify its course.

Mathematics, with all the knowledge acquired in the scientific field, can convey the development of new living species through DNA modification.

Yet the I.c. can not create new ones, it can transform them, separate them, aggregate them, but it is a dangerous game that can generate monsters.

It is undoubted that we will continue to believe in progress, but it is good to always keep in mind the fact that we can not evolve and that only our bodies have this faculty or more precisely they had it.

Differences between Evolution and Progress

Nature evolves using space, time and mass.

It is reductive to say that a stone is not alive, has its own space time and follows the same laws that govern the cells of a human brain.

Each evolutionary step is marked by an addition or a reduction.

The phrase "nothing creates, nothing is destroyed and everything is transformed" defines the meaning of evolution.

A stone, a gas, light, every particle of matter is called to define the body called the universe. The particles have a function and their space time, exactly like the cells that make up the human body, which can be defined as a small universe. It is not just an analogy but precisely the same basic language that leads to evolution.

Evolution is a condition and not a will. The world of S.u. it is conditioned by its same nature and seeks resolution. The resolution or the point of arrival of evolution is the origin or creative entity.

Nature is involuntarily attracted to the Creator and this attraction is the engine that drives evolution.

But the evolution at what point is it?

Do not confuse the world S.u. with ours. The I.c. do not exist and can only progress, for the moment the two worlds seem to have in common only the destination, not the means of transport.

Naturally the world I.c., would like to exist and then enter the world S.u.

But what would happen if this happened? In humans, for example, faculties of full control of vital functions could develop. Consciousness could order Life.exe to kill all tumor or diseased cells in the body, or in case of accidental amputation, to order regeneration of the lost limb.

Clearly the world S.u. does not perceive us and for the moment we do not run risks of rejection.

Yes, you read that correctly.

We do not exist and therefore, we can't be perceived as a threat or a resource.

Keep in mind that we are a "hierarchical structure" in a species S.u. and that theoretically, if our body evolved, abandoning this structure for another, considered more suitable, we would no longer be able to manifest ourselves.

If this happened, it would mean that I.c. is a purely coincidental event and not an evolutionary path.

Fortunately, the operating system is stable and if it is not the I.c. to genetically modify the host body, we are not at risk of extinction.

More complex, it is to understand why from the social unconsciousness we have moved to a strong individual consciousness, and not directly to the social conscience.

The world I.c. leans on the world S.u. and from it inherits part of the qualities and defects.

One condition, in particular, seems vital: intrinsic safety.

The evolutionary processes do not take longer steps than the leg, do not risk "leaps into the void", do not generate mutations that can undermine life on the planet.

In this sense, even our species should not be a leap in the dark.

The intrinsic safety protocol, continues to work for the human species, if the number of individuals on the planet were to grow and become unsustainable, nature itself would intervene, for example, with epidemic diseases.

The condition of species at the top of the food chain favors war as a final solution, regularly pursued by the same I.c. since we have manifested ourselves in the world S.u.

I want to repeat a fundamental concept that I just mentioned:

The world S.u. it does not perceive us and therefore does not implement countermeasures.

The intrinsic safety of evolutionary processes has always worked well and will always do so with every living matter.

The world S.u. generates questions and answers at the same time maintaining, in this way, the balance between all the species living on the planet.

If a species dies out, it favors a new one and the process continues.

Nature evolves and thinks of having control of the homo sapiens species, but in reality it has only the body.

This is the real critical point to examine:

If the I.c. does not exist and does not come from intrinsically safe evolutionary processes, then it can extinguish life on the planet.

For what reason the world S.u. would he have pushed himself to generate the homo sapiens?

Normally the I.c. think they are a natural evolution of life, but too many clues say the opposite.

Not just I.c. they are dangerous for life on the planet, but nature has not foreseen them.

Nature is not able to formulate questions, nevertheless we have been the umpteenth attempt to get answers.

I.c. are an answer that the world S.u. can not understand.

And here comes the borderline of the first topic discussed and the need to understand where the consciousness comes from.

Who took the first approach step?

Is it nature that has unconsciously approached consciousness, taking the evolutionary step by step, or is it the conscience that could not wait to be able to manifest itself?

In an attempt to give an answer, I.c. they have instituted, among other things, religious beliefs as well.

Unfortunately, with the passing of time, faiths have changed in cultures and political institutions.

These superstructures have undermined the credibility of the faiths and have placed them against each other.

Once the homo sapiens worshiped anything, fire, a plant, the sun.

They were amazed at everything and were respectful of creation.

We have lived a time when the search for the Creator was exciting and intellectually honest.

Then at a certain point the number of humans on the planet became too many and we began to adore each other among us, even to the point of making war.

Read and reread the sentence just written.

Evolution, in a natural way and only in the medium that it knows, places limits on living species that "widen too much" and tries to keep them in functional balance.

Evolution does not affect the number of individuals of a species, but only their qualities.

In nature everything is aimed only to return to the origin, that is, to the creative entity.

This entity some I. c. call it God, others, call it Knowledge and pursue it only through science.

I am reminded of a lion about to attack a man who is aiming it with a rifle.

The world S.u. will always attack, until extinction if necessary, only in an attempt to maintain the balance of forces in the field.

So far the evolution continues to underestimate the homo sapiens, he perceives him disarmed and helpless, with the time he saw the loss of smell, sight, muscular capacity, fur and hair, therefore, forced to cover each other's skin until cover up with oil derivatives, which crap, and now lives too longer, even if in old age.

Evolution has left homo sapiens to its fate, as a software developer would say, "upgrades are no longer planned and the system will be abandoned".

Homo sapiens is losing the evolutionary abilities of self-healing and adaptation, and now completely relies on the only power left over: progress.

I.c. have conquered a living species and the world S.u. he answered:

"You wanted the bike, now you ride it".

With only progress, we will have to face the cellular degeneration of our species: tumors, hereditary diseases, incurable diseases etc.

If in the beginning, progress and evolution, we could say synonyms, now it seems increasingly clear that we are dehumanizing, not in a derogatory sense, but in a logic of progress.

Knowledge, soon, will allow us to reach our true essence of "not living", that is, to be able to manifest ourselves also in a computer support in which the blood is replaced by electricity.

We will even exceed the limits seen in the film Matrix, no longer needing vital support, because we are not and never have been alive.

I.c. and Sex

Sex is a topic that attracts more attention than others, but it would be better to say that I.c. they are fascinated by the most powerful evolutionary weapon in the hands of the world S.u.

Eating, drinking and sleeping are natural survival functions, but to overcome the limits that guard death we must reproduce.

In the world S.u. not only is the sexual instinct the first to be born and the last to die, but it is also made pleasantly rewarding.

For their own inner equilibrium the young I.c. they approach sex for the first time through autoeroticism or masturbation.

It is absolutely the most important moment of equilibrium between the conscience and the body, and it is fundamental to understand the attitude to be taken towards "our" body.

The young I.c. they often suffer and do not interpret the evolutionary needs, and therefore I allow myself, to write some considerations that are valid both for males and for females.

There are two general autoerotic attitudes: transitive or intransitive.

If you want, introvert or extrovert.

Selfish or altruist.

The intransitive attitude leads to the satisfaction of one's need, living it almost exclusively physiologically, reaching orgasm as one gets satiety after eating.

In intransitive autoerotism, I.c. interprets sex as a utilitarian need or if you want selfish.

If consciousness has absolute control over the body up to narcissism, its weight reaches self-sufficiency and orgasm interpreted as the highest expression of self-assertion.

Love for oneself as a goal and a way of life.

In transitive autoerotism, the conscience interprets the sexual need as an opportunity for communication with our "ideal partner", even up to the condition of imagining one's own orgasm, like his.

In practice, satisfy the altruistic desire that in order to reach one's orgasm, one needs our partner to enjoy.

Transitive autoeroticism urges us to transform desire into a real relationship.

If the conscience has absolute control over the body, up to altruism, its weight reaches the emotional independence and the orgasm interpreted as maximum expression of communication.

Between these two extremes, there are infinite nuances and respective inner balances that regulate the degree of awareness.

It should be noted that however the consciousness and the body always find equilibrium, what moves is the fulcrum.

If one day you feel euphoric and the day after you are listless and depressed, it means that your I.c. can not find balance by moving the fulcrum.

This capacity depends on the degree of awareness and control of I.c. on "our body".

More precisely from the way in which I.c. has managed to "install" itself in the hardware body.

If the installation was successful, and with all the options available, you will have control and the ability to move the fulcrum.

Otherwise, your inner balance will always suffer the swing effect.

Serial killers or potential suicides and chronic depressives on the one hand, and the delirium of omnipotence on the other, are examples of excessive influence of one world on the other, without the mediation capacity allowed by moving the fulcrum.

Who is born serial killer has the predatory instinct of the world S.u. that does not separate good from evil, because for the world S.u. good and evil are a single entity.

So, no sense of guilt or almost.

Who is born fundamentally depressed, due to a partial installation of the I.c., can get to suicide as a balancing solution.

The delirium of omnipotence of I.c. can ask too much to our body and cause death in the most extreme cases.

Excessive confidence in their physical and psychological means.

Why is autoerotism so important for inner balance?

Because auto-eroticism should always be experienced before starting to have relationships with other bodies.

First we learn to understand how to satisfy our body, what we like most to imagine and think to achieve what in males, as in females, is defined orgasm.

The orgasm of autoerotism is the most intense from the purely physical point of view, in the transitive attitude, our imaginary ideal partner, will always be in symbiosis with us and will never disappoint us, in the intransitive attitude the problem does not arise.

The term autoerotism is wrong because it presupposes an activity in solitude.

In reality, the conscience and the body are two different subjects and therefore a real relationship of couple is established.

Who can live this awareness, does not suffer the loneliness of the "single".

In our society, it is more common for girls to have an attractive body.

But the speech is valid for both sexes.

If objectively our appearance is ugly, nobody will scruple to highlight it with greater or less sensitivity.

In this, as in almost all other relational cases, we are called to show a strong personality.

Accepting your body and loving yourself is essential.

If we can't do it alone, we will not convince anyone to do it for us.

Transitive autoerotism, associated with a strong balance, allows a correct degree of self-esteem.

Remember that every female or male you meet on the street, "read" your sexual attitude.

To develop sensuality, it is enough to feel sexually enjoyed.

Nobody can understand if your sexual fulfillment is due to autoeroticism or you have just finished having sex with miss or mister universe.

Being sensual means sending these non-verbal messages: "I just finished having sex but I would start again", " I like having sex, but with whom I want, and in the way I want", " I like to feel the orgasm of my partner".

An important thing to understand: it is not our partner that makes us reach orgasm.

It is always the I.c. that allows the body to enjoy, if for some reason our I.c. is not completely at ease in abandoning herself to physical pleasure, orgasm is not achieved, this also applies to males and their lack of "eiaculatio felix".

Therefore, in couple relationships, we are four, two animals and two I.c.

Do you know, two dogs that meet in the park on the leash of their owners?

Here, the relationship between the owners, is preparatory to the possibility that both decide to unleash their dogs, and to let them express their instincts.

The best sex you can do, is obtained when the conscience releases the leash, in a deliberate and conscious way, to the animal, knowing that it will return happy to its control.

Sex is the most complete means of communication that we can use as a pretext to get to know each other, and make ourselves known.

Being naked one in front of the other, should not be just an act of mutual trust, but a confirmation of the acquisition of a non-conditionable personality.

"I am naked in front of you, but I do not feel naked, because I am aware of how I am, and I love myself anyway, so it's easier for you, you can look at me with my eyes, you can see me as I see myself".

Of course, a little self-irony never disturbs, and know how to play down the embarrassments of the first few times, soften the inevitable tensions.

I.c. and Love

I have already mentioned that in the world S.u. good and evil do not exist but they are a unique force.

I.c. they reinterpreted existence through a separation, scientists are trying to understand if consciousness is the cause, or an effect.

Good and evil, in a philosophical sense, or love and hate, in a sentimental sense, define in part, who are I.c.

Let's talk about a case above all: the twin soul.

Every I.c. identifies the soul mate in a subjective way and to be able to write, you must have met one in life.

It does not matter where, how, when and why.

Only the emotions experienced are important, confirming that they are in front of the soul mate.

Depending on whether we are more animals or consciences, we can call ourselves infatuated or "in love".

If our balance has the fulcrum moved towards the animal and a more transitive auto-erotic attitude, we will easily fall in love and be conditioned by the desire to couple, naturally not only physically, because none of us is just an animal.

If we are sensual and attracted, in an evolutionary way, by our object of desire, it is easier than in our life we can meet the soul mate.

The easier we fall in love, because we like so many different types of bodies, the greater the percentage of probability that the animal that we have in front guests what we call a soul mate.

On the other hand, if we are easy to fall in love, we will not be aware of the fortune we are experiencing.

Some of us think that falling in love can not last more than two years, that the state of physiological ecstasy is consumed and reduced with the continuous cycle of sexual desire and fulfillment.

This attitude, conditioned by the evolutionary nature of the relationship, sometimes does not allow contact with the soul mate that we could have in front of us.

Keep in mind that we do not exist, so even twin souls do not exist.

The young I.c. suffer the sexual appetite and only after having satisfied the senses can find the lucidity necessary to understand if it is only sex or a relationship "in love".

What do you feel, a transitive autoerotic, in front of a soul mate?

The first sensation is a pleasant surprise, then followed by incredulous amazement, in understanding that there is no sexual desire, because simply the conscience, quickly occupies all the RAM memory, to allow Life.exe, to process a myriad of different sensations and we remain stunned.

Then the first conscious emotional responses begin.

One above all, the vivid, existential certainty of transference, then the perception of expansion of the senses, the possibility that we can manifest the Social Consciousness, perceive every movement of the creature we have before us as if it were wonderfully our own, the sensation, that also if we died at that moment, something of us would survive in her / him: the soul mate.

This is evolutionary love, not by choice but by condition.

When the soul mate is of our own sex, it is interpreted as an empathetic friendship, identical sensations themselves, except that after awareness no sexual desire appears.

Evolutionary love exists and is alive but very often, in order to live it, it must be done unconsciously.

The conscious love of I.c., is always a choice, generates different satisfactions, sex is conscious and controlled, voluntarily choosing to sacrifice some of its own liberties to have a couple relationship.

No one, including myself, can tell you what love is.

Everyone lives by reinterpreting the emotions that I have described to you, and everyone loves in a subjective way.

It also counts a certain predisposition of mind, to be able to perceive the twin souls.

The more you know yourself, the more every I.c. he must strive to move the fulcrum to his animal.

Consciousness must remain light and balanced.

Happy people have the ability to live existence knowing how to move the fulcrum between consciousness and body without ever to swing.

Of course, it is almost impossible to always succeed, but my definition of love exists between weight and counterweight.

If you have already met a soul mate, you will have already understood that your future death will not be the end of everything.

The young I.c. they do not think of death, not for exorcise it, but for evolutionary condition. If a 13-year-old thinks of his own death problem, he would do a miserable life (read: of shit).

Fortunately, evolution in this still helps us.

Unfortunately, the conscience must learn to live with nature and when an I.c. grow old, to overcome the fear of death, to have met some soul mate helps a lot.

Because the soul mate, often does not recognize us?

In practice looks at us, as if he saw a boiled fish?

In reality, if the person in front of us has a minimum of sensitivity, and in turn has had the same experience, he realizes very well that he made us "blow".

The problem is simply that we do not exist, we perceive but we can't touch, only our bodies exist and if we are not attractive, the connections are received as annoyingly disappointing.

This is because each of us would like to experience a true love story, and when we perceive that it is only on one side, we also get angry, for different reasons, on both sides.

I repeat that we do not exist and therefore we can't " join each other ".

Our bodies are alive and "merge" in sexual union much more than we can ever do with our soul mate.

Our bodies are never alone, I.c. it is isolated from the others, being able to communicate only through the living and existing body. However, we do not feel alone because we are separated but because we are not different.

Consciousness, by not existing, can perceive its presence also in another body, and this the I.c. interpret it as "soul mate", but in reality more than a transference, it is an expansion of awareness.

But then, how can we know when we love, or are we loved?

Whoever asks himself this question is always an I.c., who does not exist, who separates good from evil, who asks too many questions, who gives too many answers, who does not let his own and the other's body live. etc.etc.

Normally the most beautiful loves are those lived, the only ones that leave indelible memories.

Life.exe has saved them in our memory as "modus vivendi", because they represent us and define what we are and not what we think we are.

Knowing to love, even if it is more important than believing to love, will never be lived intensely as someone who does not know how to love, but just loves.

In your life you will meet every kind of person, and the relationship that will set up will always depend on the balance between body and I.c., example: a girl meets a boy, the girl receives signals from her female who would happily mate with the male in front of her, the I.c. of the girl naturally perceives the desire, and begins to ask it self, "I really like this here?", "Do you always dress like that?", "Why you look that girl?", "If he likes that, then is a crazed loser, or is it just a friend?".

We could go on for hours, but the meaning of the speech is that the I.c. conditions every aspect of our real life.

A girl, according to her social position or ambitions, could even inquire about the patrimonial status of who attends, or be imposed by her family.

There are always two levels in comparison: those looking for evolutionary happiness, and those who want the conscious happiness promised by progress through I.c.

When we feel happy, we are truly so until our I.c. he wonders if "we are happy", since we can't "be" we can't "be happy" and at this point the I.c. takes over and turns happiness into satisfaction, the feeling, in to common sense.

Normally, the young and very young I.c. is asked by the societies in which they are born, of learn to develop the potential that can fuel progress.

All that is taught, 99% is made for progress.

Most of us I.c. is happy in the first years of our life and then, at most, is considered "satisfied" or "serene" with the passage of time.

A small child who laughs makes us feel happy and we laugh with him.

An adult who laughs makes us ask first "why he laughs" and only then we laugh... perhaps.

How do you feel ready for a relationship of love?

How can one sexually mate in a savage and absolutely rewarding way, and immediately after having a conscientious attitude?

Understanding what conscience is is much more difficult than living with "our" body. After all, each of us is a house, and as in every house, those who live there express their own style, each of us furnishes with experience all the rooms, and each object contains a memory.

When starting a relationship with another conscience, it is very important to prevent him from moving into our inner home.

Our home represents our inner balance, and nothing must interfere between our consciousness and our body.

If this happened, it would create dependencies, sometimes so harmful, to lead to suicide, in the case of traumatic end of the relationship.

It is vitally important when we start a relationship, visualize ourselves that we lock our house, and we go out knowing that in any case, we will be able to find all our equilibrium as we have left it.

Always remember that the love between I.c. it is different from evolutionary love.

Evolutionary love is real and universal because the animal loves unconsciously.

Conscious love is a structure, and as such it builds the relationship of love from the choice of the color of the key that opens the new common home.

Some of you might think that true love and merge into a single conscious being, that nothing hides, and lives in absolute sincerity in the wake of the phrase "two hearts and a hut".

This is absolutely true for evolutionary love.

For the sake of the two I.c. agrees that both lock the respective house, and together build from scratch the "hut" of their relationship.

Always remember that we are mental "structures", and as such, we can make a backup of ourselves, build a hut with another I.c., live with it by importing everything we want to recreate from our backup, create new awareness, discover and record new ones feelings to live in love until death... else...

If things do not go, and unconsciously the relationship is already finished, before the I.c. they usually admit, it goes from a destructuring to a real destruction of the "hut", even quarreling for those who keep the useless ornaments "Dustbusters".

Believe me, knowing that you can return to your inner home, you will know how to better manage and with greater balance any experience you will be forced to live, moreover, limiting to the maximum your and others' pain.

I.c. and Politic

Even if it does not seem, the policy says a lot about what the I.c., their nature, and final destination are.

It is not politics that defines the path of progress, but the opposite, politics adapts itself to progress and does not guide it.

Consciousness is progress, and conscious progress manages I.c. and their choices. All cultures, past and present, have in common the control of society, separating the body from consciousness.

Nowadays, separation is ever more marked, and bodies are seen as vital supports for consciousness, and defined as "consumers" by economic, social and civil progress.

I.c. they are more and more conditioned by their "nature", and soon, through progress, the physical detachment between body and consciousness could take place.

You have already heard of one world government, geopolitics and energy reserves.

Many I.c. they think that behind the global project there are large lobbies and hidden powers.

Much more easily, behind the mass policies of I. c., there is our Entity, the Consciousness.

Consciousness uses scientific progress, like evolution uses nature, to find its own Entity, which objectively can be defined as "Creator" or Creative Entity.

The term God is a term I.c. that no longer means anything because it is used to support partisan convictions, or even opposed.

I.c. they are losing power in favor of Consciousness, making themselves used by Progress, and undergoing all the consequences.

I.c. they have no choice, they must progress and the term to define this process is called Provolution.

A word that does not exist, as there are no I.c., and I choose it also because it defines, in part, our superb ingenuity of gullible.

The ongoing process of dehumanization of I.c., always in a non-derogatory sense, is highlighted by the crisis of world-wide leaderism.

The Kings, Presidents or Dictators who, all over the world, at different levels, represent power over I.c., are overcome by complexity and pervasion at every level of technological progress.

I.c. they delude themselves that the control, through the information, of all the I.c. of the planet, however it is managed by other I.c., in reality it is progress itself, that becomes a system and self-feeding itself.

I.c. they press on the nature to exist, and the Conscience presses on the I.c. to expand itself and survive their death.

Politics, in general, is losing power in favor of what we call the Free Market, which has very little free.

But what really unites all the I.c. on the planet, is the money exchange market.

Who manages the coins, manages the policies of each nation, and all the I.c. they are controlled by a system, which they themselves believe they have chosen. In reality it is the Provolution that has chosen, as the most suitable tool for its purposes, financial mathematics. Naturally, there are pockets of resistance in the society of I. c. which oppose the commodification of every natural aspect of our life.

Our destiny is not marked, but we are in the hands of the Provolution which really defines what we are becoming and traces the path of this trend.

Local policies are "background noises", even wars between nations or ethnic groups, they hide, the true motivations of the succession of events. Individually every I.c. generates a Provolutive cycle.

Example: I decide to eat three times a day, at the same time, to sleep at night, to stay awake during the day.

This micro cycle, linked to a choice of a single I.c., is the basic element of every macro cycle of I.c.

The most famous cycle known, and the most important, is the life-death cycle.

From this cycle is built, and depends, any other cycle.

In economics, in mathematics, in gardening, in politics, all cycles depend on the duration of a single life, in support of each single I.c.

In the last few centuries, the average life span of a human being has gone from 40 to 80 years, I don't want to be precise in age, just because it is irrelevant for the example.

All the cycles, which pertain to any activity of the I.c., are lengthened, this implies that there are no perfect or mathematical cycles, that is, that an event is repeated with a regular expiration.

For example, in financial mathematics, cycles are often used to try to predict stock market movements, but it is not true that every 7 years there is a collapse or every 5 years a new price increase.

In evolution all cycles influence one another in existential harmony.

In Provolution, all the cycles generated by the presence I.c., tend to perfection, but using simplified tools such as the decimal system in mathematics.

On the whole planet, there are not two human beings eating three times a day, at the same time, the same quantity, the same things.

Only Provolution tends to make perfect cycles exist, but as stated in this book, consciousness does not exist, and Provolution, for the moment, is always beaten by evolutionary reality.

Politics too has a cyclical structure, and its choices influence the cycles of peace and war, economic expansion and contraction, affirmation and denial of reality.

For many I.c., the Provolutive cycle in politics is unacceptable, they believe that progress, from anarchy, to dictatorship, to democracy, is a linear process and that political choices always tend to improve the societies that manage.

In reality, politics is always a utopia, that is, the ideal desire to achieve something good and just, applies only in a Provolutive environment, but it never faithfully applies to the cyclical reality of evolution, which, as already pointed out, has no perception of the existence of the I.c.

More the I.c. they insist in wanting, for example, a continuous economic growth, or of democratic rights, or in generic terms of Provolution, the more the evolutionary reality realigns in violent way.

Example: if I was born into a democratic regime or a dictatorship, my generation has not known other social regimes, it is therefore more difficult, that develops an evolutionary-regenerative cycle that puts into question the status quo.

However, the status quo is Provolutive, and like the Holy Roman Empire is finished, it will also end the dictatorial regime of North Korea, but not because it is an unjust or wrong regime, but because it is conditioned to the evolutionary reality.

Also in this sense, evolution is a safety valve for some I.c., while for others I.c., it is a limit to be overcome with the Provolution.

I can give you for sure, that in our future there will be the one world government, but in what form and substance, if democratic or dictatorial, its duration will depend on the respect it will have of evolutionary cycles.

I.c. and Singularity

At every birth, the Consciousness must start all over again.

It can manifest itself as I.c. but it does not remember anything of the previous existences.

While evolution writes what has been in the cells, and passes it on to the new generations, I.c. they went from graffiti to rocks, to books, to data servers.

I.c. they have a huge hunger for memory, to be able to register acquired knowledge.

The dream of the Consciousness is, to manifest itself in an I.c., to know everything that has been learned in generations, and therefore to be able to pass it on to the offspring as the evolution.

Will it ever happen?

By logic, it would seem so, because it has already happened in the past, and precisely with the emergence of the first I.c. in our ancestors.

Suppose that in any living species, even by mistake or defect, a genetic mutation occurs, in this case of "reduction", if it were a modification made by chemical thought on the reproductive cells, it would be "adduction".

Evolution can only make adduction changes, if not, it could to involve, the reduction is synonymous of extinction or "death risk".

Example: a lizard is born without paws, if it wants to survive, it must adapt, crawl like a snake and feed itself.

If it finds an existential balance, it can try to reproduce itself, if it finds an available companion, it could give birth to a certain number of lizards without paws, that by coupling with each other, could make a variant of the same species permanent.

Normally this does not happen, changes due to reduction lead to death and not to a progenitor.

However, this process could explain the manifestation of I.c. in our ancestors.

At the appearance of the patient zero, as a virologist would call him, his fellows might have taken him for weird, absent, distracted, one who "thought too much".

To born with the I.c., it is not like being born without paws, and survival has obviously been assured.

My hypothesis is that I.c., is an adaptation response to a genetic modification of reduction, intervened in chemical thought at the time of cellular writing, precisely of the information needed to generate the brain.

But why reductive genetics, and not adductive?

By exclusion, the facts tell us that in other species does not develop consciousness, evidently, because evolution, normally, gives coherent changes.

Do not misinterpret my words, I'm not saying that the I.c. are a mistake, but if we are a randomness, it is better for our good that it remains unrepeatable for this planet.

If it is true that history repeats itself in a cyclical form, even if in always different variations, it means that even today, there are I.c. with particular faculties, or difficulties, which may have opened a window on our entity: the Conscience.

To give some examples: the shamans, Jesus, Muhammad, the mediums, the empathists, the geniuses, Padre Pio, Natuzza Evolo etc. etc. I put them in random order because they still lack lists of those living and recognized as important and genuine.

Of these I.c. living or lived, strikes a resemblance: all, depending on the place and society of origin, develop a coherent language, that is, to shaman, to Muhammad we would hardly have seen the stigmata appear.

The Consciousness is pressing on the I.c., when and if the Indigo children will be reality, then we will approach the S.c., that is, Social Conscience.

For those who do not know, Indigo children are the new generations who develop particular empathic or precognitive qualities.

Then?

When an I.c. of this type will become the progenitor, perhaps we will have humanity 2.0, until then we try not to extinguish humanity 1.0 and we with it.

Intrinsic capacities S.u.
vs.
Extrinsic capacities I.c.

It would seem an impossible fight in favor of the I.c., and yet, there are capacity S.u. unmatchable.

One of these is synchronized swimming, which I take as an example to underline that the S.u. and evolutionary chemical thinking dominates, in many respects.

To obtain the perfection of the movements of a shoal of sardines, I.c. they have to study and swim together years.

There are no road signs or traffic lights in the anthills, but the traffic is always fluid. Imagine a city without street names, traffic lights, or satellite navigators.

The energy that the world S.u. uses to exist, is infinitesimal compared to that necessary to the world of I.c., lately we have discovered correlations between oil extractions and earthquakes, but already using common sense, we could guess that by removing something at a depth of two / three kilometers, you provoke a depression that, sooner or later, the earth's crust tends to compensate.

Human activities on the planet are much less efficient than those of nature, whose parameters are intrinsically very high, because they are united by an extremely binding evolutionary process.

Unfortunately, the I.c. tend to extrapolate from the context, the goals achieved by progress, not being able to connect the dots of the Provolutive scheme, which we currently suffer, rather than managing it.

The world of S.u. unconsciously moves in a collective way, the world I.c. it moves consciously in a scattered order, and selfishly individual.

If you are not going to give yourself to synchronized swimming, I can suggest a trick to find out if you can expand your knowledge.

Learn from yourselves, tricking your brain into believing that him already know things.

It's a small expedient that all students already know, but I want to explain how it works.

You have to give an exam, any examination, and you have little memory for topics that do not interest you, and have been explained by a teacher with a shrill voice or a professor with a tone of voice that facilitates the lethargy.

You have to implement a "reverse engineering".

Normally, each of us thinks with our own voice, our brain elaborates the thought, and translates it simultaneously, making it available to our I.c. in what can be defined as our personal "machine language", which requires the least amount of resources to achieve maximum efficiency.

What makes it so fast, is our voice, what we hear coming out of our head, not the one recorded with a microphone, yes, we know it's ours, but we do not feel like that.

Get a voice synthesizer, even just software, try to tune your voice with the one coming out of the speakers, if you're lucky, it might be enough to adjust the high and low tones.

The more you are fussy, the more your "machine language" will be effective.

Now, all you have to do is record the exam text, having the foresight to follow these indications: you must read without hesitation or reasoning pauses, in a clear and fluid way, as if they were words conceived and elaborated by your brain and exits from your mouth.

Put yourself in the headphones, and listen to what you know.

Even without concentrating, your brain will receive these notions as their own, and will record them as flashbacks, that is, as a memory recalled by deep memory, that ROM, the consolidated one, not that RAM, waiting for processing, which could then be forgotten.

This method is excellent for learning a language and it's pronunciation with the same attentions.

Buy a reduced English / Italian dictionary and try to assimilate it by simply reading it.

Do not read "amore means love" or "casa means home", your brain does not think so, but instantly translates the word it knows, so you have to read "amore love" and "casa home", leaving only a little more time, between a couple of words and the other.

But the most important thing is to read the translation with emphasis, as if you already knew, and with tone from "this I already know".

I.c. and Food

Food is all that can be eaten and digested, even glass or poison.

This is the definition of food for the Provolution.

In an evolutionary sense, food is all that is natural, and not contaminated by the intervention I.c.

The food chain, which defines the relationships between the different living species, is the yardstick that evolution uses to define what is food and what is not.

Colonizing the brain of an animal, the I.c. managed to move it to the top of the food chain, snatching it from the jaws of natural predators.

This advancement at the top of the food chain is not the only move that I.c. it has provoked in the evolutionary rules, it is said that every living species is food for another.

In the evolutionary rules are also contemplated the ways, and the times, of death.

You can die as food, by hunger, old age, sickness or accidentally.

I.c. they added other types of deaths, the most trivial, it is useless death, the one caused by fun or just by the will to do it.

To a S.u. like the cat, it can happen that you play educatively with the life of a mouse, catch it, hold it by its tail, release it and recapture it, but if it is not hungry, the death of the prey may be accidental or finalized.

Accidental, if the recapture is excessively violent, but often, if the capture is not aimed at satiety, the prey is left to escape, without further pursuit.

Finalized, teaching or learning and not infrequently behavioral, when interacting with an I.c., leaving the mouse's head on the threshold of house.

I used an animal as an example, to underline the conditionings I.c. in the world S.u.

Normally, in evolution, death by suicide is always induced, whereas for I.c. it is always voluntary.

The most sneaky type of death, which the I.c. added to the evolutionary list, is the "non-death" or "existential oblivion".

Imagine a lion falling into a crevasse, isolated from water and preys to eat, his fate is marked, and death comes so quickly, the more energy the lion spends, to try to climb, in the attempts, he continues to fall, hurts himself, and accelerates the moment of death.

Despite the evolution follows strict rules, it never rages beyond measure, always keeping in natural balance, the relationship between life and death, uniting them together, because they are the same thing.

They are the I.c. who interpret life and death, separated by the time between the two events: birth and death.

Social Unconsciousness does not need to compare with the time, because it is not aware of it, is the time that manifests itself as a measure of the evolution.

Another topic.

A classic "non-death" are the zoos, animals enclosed in cages, artificially fed by I.c., a complete evolutionary nonsense, where a S.u. it is broken, separated from evolution and its laws.

Other "not death" classic, are the intensive farms, animals used as humans food. "Non-living" beings for the evolution.

In principle, even the so-called animals of affection, such as dogs, cats, turtles, rabbits, horses etc.etc. they are, to varying degrees, removed from the evolutionary rules, and the more they are connected empatically to an I.c., the more they become dependent, sometimes to the point of making conflictual, the relationship between the world I.c. and the world of S.u.

Dogs chained, who bite to kill the children of the owners, animals that let themselves die of hunger, cats that launch from the terrace of the fifth floor, are just extreme examples, but still evident, the complex and complicated relationship between the two worlds.

The food in the world S.u. it is environmental, and every living species eats, is eaten, the predator of one is the prey of another, in the world I.c. the food is unrecognizable, having become a product composed of other I.c., they often declare, "I would never eat it, not even dead".

The I.c. have lost the evolutionary faculties to understand if the food they have before them is edible, moreover, even the foods that we recognize as plants or animals, could be treated with additives or genetically modified.

Even vegetables grown in gardens and apparently natural could be contaminated with harmful fertilizers, and therefore food depends on trust in other people.

The food has therefore been distorted, removed from the evolutionary processes, from quality control to intrinsic safety, guaranteed by the world S.u.

Naturally the speech is only to detect the risks connected to the activities of the I.c. and in general, to the pollution they have caused in the evolutionary processes.

For pollution, therefore, it is not meant only the environmental, but more dangerous and pernicious, the meaning of the word "progress" in form and substance, as a synonym.

Progress is the pollutant of the S.u. world, it modifies its values and qualities, it generates vegetable and animal hybrids that would be destined for extinction without the intervention of the I.c., even through a selection or an environmental modification, the evolutionary laws are bent to the Provolutive interest.

Evolutionary saturation
vs.
Provolutive expansion

Evolutionary saturation is evidenced by a slowing of the speed in the generation of new living species.

On planet earth, after a very long gestation period, a few million years ago, thanks to oxygen, life, as we know it now, found the means to expand rapidly.

The gestation period wrote the rules that allowed to unlock the evolutionary constraints conditioned by the previous status quo.

Let us remember that even a stone is potentially alive.

Time and movement are not a problem for the S.u. world, matter is enough, its potential energy, and sooner or later, the stone can be transformed into a butterfly.

This has happened and life has colonized the planet, taking advantage of all possible development opportunities.

And now? Now life struggles and defends positions, inherent evolutionary laws slow down self-regeneration and prevent self-destruction.

In this environment also appeared the I.c., perhaps, as one of the many attempts, by the evolution, to continue to expand even undergoing techniques of reduction at risk of extinction, of which I have already mentioned.

The birth of I.c. in this context, has allowed a relief valve to the evolutionary pressures, which is evident, could never expand beyond the confines of the planet.

I wrote that evolution is on its way to the origin from which it all began, the point of creation, the creative force or God, in religious terms.

I guess each of us has wondered why the laws of physics are what they are, and they have put thousands of light years away between one planet and another.

In all these planets, they are less or more evolved than our, saturation is dealt with, and the status quo once again be overcome, perhaps thanks to the birth of I.c. and the writing of new Provolutive rules, suitable for facing interstellar and intergalactic journeys.

Personally I think that our nature will remain on this planet and the great journey will be faced by conscious computers that will transport our genetic heritage around the universe, looking for a hospitable planet to colonize, however also the consolidated idea of spaceships at Star Trek, it's not bad.

Evolutionary saturation pushes frontier solutions.

Imagine the universe as a plant and the big-bang as its roots, the trunk and the branches like space and matter, with its billions of galaxies, up to its flowers, and the planets saturated with life.

Our planet has flourished and continues to flourish, but its fruits are only partly generated to feed itself.

The cycle must close with the fruit that falls and returns to the roots, the seeds transported, are us I.c.

If as I believe, the world S.u. it has inescapable evolutionary rules, then the structure of the existing is applicable in all its parts, either in the infinitely large, like the universe, or in the dimensions of a planet.

La Provolution is our ripening fruit and no fruit remains attached to the plant forever, sooner or later, the seeds are released.

I.c. and Time

Consciousness does not age and everything that does not age does not exist.

The hierarchical structure of cells in our brain never decays, what degenerates is the set of cells that compose it, for old age, for diseases like senile dementia or vascular stroke.

Whether you are six or ninety years old, I.c. it manifests itself fully thanks to its structure.

A stone ages because it simply has a mass and is therefore subjected to gravitational force and potential which, over an infinite time, consume it by modifying it and transforming it.

Our body suffers the same forces, but clearly, to die, it takes much less effort, ours is called "Time Limit", and is defined with the DNA structure of our species.

As much as we can eat and drink healthy, sleep well, do physical activity, or slow down our metabolism to save energy, we can't exceed the organic cells limit and their decay.

But this is true in evolution, if you are a feline like the puma, you will move very quickly to nourish yourself by consuming a lot of energy, your accelerated metabolism will dictate the time limit of your life.

If you are a plant, you can live centuries but even a turtle does not joke longevity.

In nature, therefore, there is a relationship between time, movement and metabolism.

These relationships change of value for each living species and determine the "Time Limit".

I.c. are hosted in human bodies and through the Provolution, will continue to lengthen the time limit with the specific purpose of helping the Conscious to manifest, or anyway, to find a way to overcome the limits.

But what is the relationship between time and conscience?

Consciousness and time do not exist, one is timeless and the other is a relative measure, and both manifest.

Consciousness and time derive from the creative entity, or at least they are very close to the mystery of creation.

Time, as a measure, exists only for I.c. and their concept of simplification of reality, for the world S.u. time is identified with mass and movement.

It is good to understand that the world S.u. it is already present throughout the universe, on every more or less vital planet, precisely because of the medium it has always used, that is evolution.

Clearly, Social Unconsciousness can't know that it exists, but it exists everywhere, those who need to find themselves are those who do not exist and try to find themselves looking for themselves everywhere.

The Provolutive push will not stop, and has already passed some limits of evolution, of which, the time factor, was precursor.

The consciousness of passing time, determines imminence and apprehensive action, the I.c. knowing that they can stop manifest itself, they spur movement and research.

Looking for evidence throughout the universe, of one's existence, certifies with what anxiety the I.c. "they don't living" their condition.

I.c. and Existential Anxiety

I.c. they always think they exist, and for them, this is an incontrovertible fact, and yet they suffer existential anxiety with statements like: "What will you do when you grow up?", "Do not waste time", "remember, life is one", "today you're here tomorrow, who knows!" and the most famous "remember that you have to die!".

What identifies consciousness is the Doubt value of which I mentioned earlier. In the world S.u. doubt does not exist because he can not ask questions to himself, if the male of the Black Widow asks himself why he will be eaten alive by the female, evolution would not exist as we know it now.

The instillation of Doubt in I.c. provokes wars, condominium fights and sloth to the limit case, of death by starvation, when it is such that it blocks movement, the choice.

In religion, doubt is synonymous with lack of faith.

Doubt is an integral part of consciousness, and is perhaps the daughter of evolutionary saturation, a response for "reduction", to an evolutionary bottleneck.

I.c. more aware, they are more afraid of physical pain than of the moment of death, in the world of S.u. death is very often violent and painful, but the fact that there is no concept of acceptance or rebellion, makes life, death, pain, pleasure, good, evil, all synonymous.

No doubt, no question, pure existence.

I.c. they have doubts, questions, need answers.

This moves them away from existence itself, both in a material and philosophical sense, and Provolution can fuel the emotional depression that certifies the evident inability to exist.

The emotional depression from "existential anxiety" is another indication that the I.c. does not exist.

I hope you young I.c., you never have to confront a beast so ferocious as depression, who did it and it came out victorious, it still bears the signs.

Arm yourselves therefore with the awareness that you do not "exist", surely it does not make things worse.

Being doubtful is part of our inner condition, we can not evade it and the anxiety of living that we experience, in the attempt to affirm our existence, can be used to know us from an alternative point of view..

The phrases "being detached" or "seeing things in perspective", acquire a more realistic meaning if we accept that consciousness does not exist.

It is like getting rid of a burden, the children you will have will be your body but will have nothing of your conscience.

It is not by having children, that you can leave something of you, in heredity, writing books, painting pictures, composing sonnets, they are examples of means of transitive witness more suitable, if you really want to leave something to posterity.

Some I.c. it leaves financial empires, other established companies, others simply a home for their children.

What appears evident, is that every I.c. leaves something that can be traced back to the concept of "structure".

Whenever an I.c. he dies, he leaves a part of what he thinks he is, but he is not, and everything can be traced back to a different form of "structure".

All the activities of consciousness have a "formal structure" modeled on the "material substance", but the substance exists, the form does not.

Existential anxiety feeds on the fact that I.c. they can not reproduce, and at every birth, they start all over again, but this condition could lead to another Provolutive step.

Incredibly every I.c. it could really die, in case the conscience could transfer its experience.

Now, whenever I meet a friend or cross the gaze of a child, I recognize my own I.c. formed with different experiences but with the same structural Consciousness, but everything would change if I met an I.c. 2.0 that recalls his previous experiences.

the I.c. 1.0 would become extinct like the Neanderthal man.

For the moment every I.c. it is a relatively immortal structure that continues to be reborn, constantly repeating different Provolutive processes, to overcome its limits.

In this, the evolution and the Provolution have a point of contact.

Possible answers
to
Questions never asked

How did the idea of writing a book on conscience come about?

The idea was to write a book for the pleasure of doing it, immediately afterwards the choice of the topic came.

In my mind, everything was focused, from motivation, to the means at my disposal in dealing with a subject in which I had experience and of which I could write.

By exclusion, I realized that it was the same "ability to choose", to be an argument.

The consequent passage led straight to the conscience and its meaning.

But from this, to thinking that consciousness does not exist, is the passage so short?

The same capacity that each of us has, to write and communicate, to choose between a no and a yes, or to do one thing instead of another, has led me to wonder, not only who I was, but how I "worked", the questions in my mind increased instead of diminishing, the answers I could process seemed logical and definitive, but then other questions crept up the doubt of the existence of my conscience, and the doubt itself had become the only answer.

If consciousness does not exist on the physical plane, how can there not be a destabilizing impact on the practical level?

I think that a possible answer is the consideration, that the consciousness works in a bidirectional way, and the mind in a unidirectional way towards a thing that does not exist and is not perceived, a bit like a virus in the computer.

Conscience makes choices, imposes them on our animal mind that is not able to respond positively or negatively, implements them as if they were his.

An animal mind works for both internal and external stimuli, but it is not able to extrapolate them from the context of cause and effect.

Also the degree of intelligence is conditioned to the evolutionary laws.

In this environment, conscious intelligence creeps in, or more precisely, its "disguise virus".

Consciousness does not make our animal brain smarter, in reality, the processing processes are identical to those of other species.

Consciousness has colonized the hominid brain and has replaced the unconscious mental impulses with its own, until it becomes the homo sapiens - sapiens that we recognize.

Incredibly, if consciousness ceased to manifest itself, homo sapiens - sapiens would prove, due to atrophy, the stupidest beast on the planet and would quickly die out, having no time to readjust to the evolutionary conditions.

Assuming that consciousness does not exist, what could we or should we do differently than before?

Nothing. The implications concern only our perception of reality and, in practice, our capacity for inner balance.

For what I think, and I have argued, I can say that, for example, I do not have "faith in the Creator".

I have the certainty that the "Creator exists" and I do not feel the "need" to believe in any religious institution.

Among other things, what so many I.c. they believe in the manifestation of God incarnate, or his ascetic testimonies, are irrelevant for me, that is, they do not remove or add anything to my conviction of the existence of the Creator.

If I had to point out an orientation of intent, I would recommend to every young I.c. to reason with one's own conscience, without preconceptions, and return to explore all the things that are taken for granted, taking into account our "non-existence".

Many scientists are already engaged on these issues, but what does this text add to the ongoing research?

This is just a book that tries to highlight points of deepening. In part it is provocative, but it is written in a discursive and simple way, avoiding to appear simplistic.

I have not intentionally made references to texts and thesis of authoritative signatures, from which I could find support or contrast. The spirit of the book is to encourage oneself to search for oneself and to grow in awareness.

How can the statement that consciousness does not exist, help people live better?

The two things are not connected by cause and effect.

Try to prove that consciousness does not exist, it allows to explore its origin from different points of view.

Happiness, like other goals, could be brought into focus by one of these points.

What are the conclusions to be drawn, on such a complex subject, as the theory of non-existence of consciousness?

Difficult to answer. These are many small clues that must be evaluated individually and collectively.

The effects of the theory on reality can only modify the method of approach to the themes, faced by the conscience, not the results.

The conscience appears strongly linked to its origin, many I.c. they believe they are descended from the divine and therefore at the origin of existence.

Others I.c. they think that once dead, it's all over, and you do not go back.

Looking for other conceptual paths, it favors the discovery of the processes that can circumscribe the identity, that is, the nature of the doubt, from which springs every existential position of the single I.c.

In mathematics, the dubitative value does not exist, the closest one is the random value.

In reality, the random value is still potentially scalable because it is physically generated by a chip and its internal clock machine.

Through reverse engineering, theoretically, the random process can be reproduced.

The dubitative value can be imagined as a new number, outside the decimal scale, outside the box, I call it Phantom.

If consciousness has a root, Phantom could be the key to identifying it in a mathematical structure.

I have already mentioned that prime numbers tend to be linked, in some way, to using the number zero.

It is good to remember that the decimal system is a simplified system, probably, implement the Phantom number, would make more complete the understanding of advanced mathematics.

Naturally the Phantom is a purely speculative number.

I understand that these last statements are very difficult, to return to a simpler topic, I re-mention the choices that have the I.c. to worry more about our body or more of our Entity, the Consciousness.

In principle, plus an I.c. takes care of his body, plus the other I.c. understand and share.

When an I.c. deals with his Conscience, the other I.c. they contrast and fragment, demonstrating perfectly their individual nature.

Not only in politics, but also in personal relationships, words are used to affirm "their own" ideas, and not just to affirm ideas.

The ideas and opinions are all personal, if they can have a monetary value, a position value, or a political value.

Ideas become common and shareable, only when for I.c. forgiveness of personal interest.

This attitude has become a system with all material goods, there is nothing on the planet that has not been priced, but more and more, the so-called market, is interested in pricing the mental and behavioral activities of people.

Evolutionary saturation exists, but the Provolutive saturation processes need to be deepened to understand, how and when, can manifest themselves signs of conflict between our bodies and I.c.

So far the Provolution has also worked for our bodies, if it goes further, many I.c. they will choose to ally with evolution by opening completely new scenarios.

From wars managed by the I.c. between different bodies, to wars managed between different I.c. for the same bodies.

Hallucinating, right!?

Good conscience to all...
and study yourself!

SUMMARY

Special thanks:
dedicated to all those who support me
and those who can't stand me